Updated Netherlands Travel Guide

Lucas Everhart

Updated Netherlands Travel Guide

Updated Netherlands Travel Guide

A Comprehensive Guide to Explore the Rich History, iconic tourist spots, Natural Wonders, Vibrant Culture, and Stunning Landscapes of Netherlands and Travel Tips from Locals

By

Lucas Everhart

Copyright © Lucas Everhart [2023]

All rights reserved. No part of this book may be reproduced, stored in a retrieval system, or transmitted in any form or by any means, electronic, mechanical, photocopying, recording, or otherwise, without the prior written permission of the copyright owner.

Disclaimer:

The information provided in this book, "Updated Netherlands Travel Guide," is for general informational purposes only. While I have made every effort to ensure the accuracy and timeliness of the information, I do not make any representations or warranties of any kind, express or implied, about the completeness, accuracy, reliability, suitability, or availability of the information contained in this guide. Any reliance you place on such information is strictly at your own risk.

The book serves as a guide and should not substitute professional advice or serve as a guarantee of the conditions, safety, or quality of the destinations, accommodations, services, or activities mentioned. I disclaim any liability for any loss, injury, or inconvenience sustained by any reader as a result of the information or advice presented in this book.

It is recommended that readers independently verify and confirm any important information, such as visa requirements, health and safety guidelines, and local laws and regulations, before traveling to Netherlands. The author shall not be held

Updated Netherlands Travel Guide

liable for any inaccuracies or changes in the information provided.

Updated Netherlands Travel Guide

Table of Content

Table of Content 6
Introduction 10
    Why You Should Visit the Netherlands 13
    About This Guide 15
Planning Your Trip 18
    Best Time to Visit 19
    Visa Requirements and Travel Documents 21
    Health and Safety Tips 23
    Budgeting and Money Matters 25
    Getting Around the Netherlands 28
Exploring Amsterdam 30
    Top Attractions and Landmarks 32
    Museums and Galleries 34
    Canals and Boat Tours 37
    Parks and Outdoor Activities 39
    Shopping and Markets 42
    Dining and Nightlife 44
        Dining 44
        Nightlife 45
Beyond Amsterdam: Highlights of the Netherlands 48
    Rotterdam 50
    The Hague 52
    Utrecht 54

Updated Netherlands Travel Guide

Maastricht	56
Groningen	58
Haarlem	61
Delft	63
Leiden	66
Dutch Culture and Traditions	68
History of the Netherlands	71
Dutch Art and Architecture	74
Festivals and Events	77
Cuisine and Local Delicacies	79
Language and Etiquette	81
Outdoor Adventures	84
Cycling in the Netherlands	85
Hiking and Nature Reserves	87
Water Sports and Beaches	89
National Parks and Gardens	91
Practical Information	94
Accommodation Options	96
Local Transportation	98
Communication and Internet Access	100
Shopping Tips and VAT Refunds	102
Useful Phrases and Translations	104
Insider Tips and Hidden Gems	106
Off-the-Beaten-Path Destinations	108
Unique Experiences in the Netherlands	110

Updated Netherlands Travel Guide

Conclusion..112

Updated Netherlands Travel Guide

Introduction

The Netherlands, often called Holland, is a vibrant and culturally rich country in Northwestern Europe. Known for its picturesque landscapes, windmills, tulip fields, and canals, the Netherlands offers a unique blend of history, art, and modernity. With a population of over 17 million people, the country may be small in size, but it packs a big punch when it comes to attractions and experiences.

One of the country's most famous cities is Amsterdam, the capital and largest city of the Netherlands. Amsterdam is renowned for its elaborate canal system, charming narrow houses, and world-class museums. Visitors can explore the historic Anne Frank House, the Van Gogh Museum, and the Rijksmuseum, which houses masterpieces by Rembrandt and Vermeer. The city's vibrant atmosphere is further enhanced by its lively nightlife, trendy neighborhoods, and diverse culinary scene.

Updated Netherlands Travel Guide

Beyond Amsterdam, the Netherlands is home to several other captivating cities and towns. Rotterdam, known for its modern architecture, is a bustling port city with an innovative spirit. The Hague, the seat of the Dutch government, offers a rich blend of politics, history, and culture. Utrecht, with its charming canals and medieval city center, is a vibrant university town. These cities, along with Maastricht, Groningen, Haarlem, Delft, and Leiden, each have their own unique character and attractions, making them worth exploring.

The Netherlands is renowned for its extensive network of well-maintained cycling paths, making it a paradise for cyclists. Biking through the countryside, past colorful tulip fields, charming villages, and lush green landscapes, is a quintessentially Dutch experience. The country's flat terrain makes it easy for both locals and visitors to hop on a bike and explore at their own pace.

Dutch culture is deeply rooted in history and traditions. The Netherlands has been a global trade and economic powerhouse for centuries, and this heritage is reflected in its art, architecture, and cuisine. The Dutch Masters, including Rembrandt and Vermeer, has left an indelible mark on the world of art. Traditional Dutch dishes like stroopwafels, herring, and cheese are a delight for food lovers.

The Netherlands is also known for its progressive and inclusive society. It has a reputation for being environmentally conscious and innovative, with sustainable initiatives and a focus on renewable energy.

The Netherlands offers a fascinating blend of history, culture, and natural beauty. From the iconic canals of Amsterdam to the windmills of Kinderdijk, there is something to enchant every visitor. Whether you're exploring the vibrant cities, cycling through the countryside, or immersing yourself in Dutch art and culture, the Netherlands promises a memorable and enriching travel experience.

Why You Should Visit the Netherlands

There are countless reasons why you should visit the Netherlands. From its picturesque landscapes to its rich cultural heritage, the country offers a wide range of experiences that will leave you with unforgettable memories. Here are a few compelling reasons to add the Netherlands to your travel bucket list.

First and foremost, the Netherlands is renowned for its charming cities and towns. Amsterdam, the capital city, is a vibrant metropolis known for its stunning canal network, historic architecture, and world-class museums. From the iconic Anne Frank House to the Van Gogh Museum, there are countless cultural treasures to explore. Additionally, cities like Rotterdam, The Hague, and Utrecht offer their own unique attractions and atmospheres, showcasing modern architecture, royal palaces, and lively cultural scenes.

Another reason to visit the Netherlands is its natural beauty. The country's countryside is a patchwork of tulip fields, windmills, and picturesque villages. Exploring these landscapes on a bicycle or by taking a leisurely canal cruise is a delightful way to immerse yourself in the Dutch scenery. The Netherlands is also home to numerous national parks, such as Hoge Veluwe National Park, where you can encounter diverse flora and fauna while enjoying hiking or cycling trails.

The Dutch are renowned for their progressive and inclusive society. The Netherlands is a global leader in sustainable practices, with initiatives focused on renewable energy, eco-friendly transportation, and environmental conservation. Exploring this forward-thinking mindset can be both inspiring and educational.

The Netherlands offers a vibrant cultural scene. From world-class art museums to music festivals and street markets, there is always something happening in the country. Dutch cuisine, including delicious cheeses, stroopwafels, and herring, is a treat for food enthusiasts. The Dutch also celebrate various festivals throughout the year, showcasing their rich traditions and cultural diversity.

The Netherlands offers a unique blend of cultural heritage, natural beauty, and progressive values. Whether you're strolling along Amsterdam's canals, exploring the countryside by bike, or immersing yourself in Dutch art and cuisine, the Netherlands promises a captivating and enriching travel experience.

Updated Netherlands Travel Guide

About This Guide

Welcome to the "Updated Netherlands Travel Guide"! This comprehensive guide is designed to be your ultimate companion as you explore the beautiful country of the Netherlands. Whether you're a first-time visitor or a seasoned traveler, this guide aims to provide you with all the essential information, insider tips, and recommendations to make your trip unforgettable.

This guide has been carefully curated and updated to ensure that you have the most up-to-date and relevant information about the Netherlands. I have taken into account the latest travel trends, new attractions, and changes in the country's infrastructure, so you can plan your trip with confidence.

Inside this guide, you will find detailed sections on planning your trip, including the best time to visit, visa requirements, health and safety tips, and budgeting advice. I have also included practical information on getting around the Netherlands, including local transportation options and communication services, to help you navigate the country with ease.

To help you make the most of your time in the Netherlands, I have dedicated sections to the top cities and attractions. From Amsterdam, Rotterdam, and The Hague to lesser-known gems like Utrecht, Maastricht, and Delft, we provide in-depth information on the must-visit places, iconic landmarks, museums, and cultural experiences that each city offers.

Moreover, this guide goes beyond the popular destinations and uncovers hidden gems, off-the-beaten-path locations, and unique experiences that will allow you to delve deeper into the Dutch culture and lifestyle. I believe that exploring these lesser-known places will provide you with a more authentic and memorable travel experience.

In addition to practical and sightseeing information, this guide also delves into the rich cultural heritage of the Netherlands. You will find insights into Dutch history, art, traditions, festivals, cuisine, and language, allowing you to fully immerse yourself in the local culture.

Throughout this guide, you will discover insider tips, recommended itineraries, and useful resources to help you plan and execute your trip smoothly. I want this guide to be your go-to resource, providing you with all the necessary information to make your journey through the Netherlands an incredible adventure.

So, grab your copy of the "Updated Netherlands Travel Guide" and get ready to embark on a memorable journey through this fascinating country. Let this guide be your trusted companion as you explore the enchanting cities, charming landscapes, and vibrant culture of the Netherlands.

Updated Netherlands Travel Guide

PLANNING YOUR TRIP

When planning your trip to the Netherlands, there are a few key factors to consider. Start by choosing the best time to visit based on your preferences, whether it's the vibrant tulip season in spring or the festive atmosphere during the summer. Be aware of the visa requirements and ensure you have the necessary travel documents.

It's essential to prioritize health and safety by checking any travel advisories and arranging travel insurance. Create a budget, considering accommodation, transportation, and attractions. Finally, familiarize yourself with the efficient transportation system to easily navigate the country and make the most of your time in the Netherlands.

Updated Netherlands Travel Guide

Best Time to Visit

The Netherlands offers something unique in every season, so the best time to visit depends on your preferences and the experiences you seek. Here's a breakdown of the different seasons and what they offer:

- **Spring (March to May):** Springtime in the Netherlands is renowned for its vibrant tulip fields, particularly in April and early May. Keukenhof Gardens near Amsterdam is a must-visit during this time, where you can witness millions of blooming flowers. The weather is generally mild, making it perfect for outdoor activities and exploring the cities.
- **Summer (June to August):** The summer months bring pleasant temperatures, with highs ranging from 20 to 25 degrees Celsius (68 to 77 degrees Fahrenheit). It's a popular time for tourists, especially in July and August when the weather is warmest. You can enjoy outdoor festivals, street markets, and open-air concerts. The long daylight hours allow for more time to explore the cities and enjoy outdoor activities like cycling and boating.
- **Autumn (September to November):** Autumn in the Netherlands offers beautiful foliage, particularly in parks and forests. The temperatures start to cool down, but it remains relatively mild. This season is ideal for visiting museums and galleries, as well as attending cultural events and exhibitions.

- **Winter (December to February):** The Netherlands experiences cold winters, with temperatures ranging from 2 to 6 degrees Celsius (36 to 43 degrees Fahrenheit). However, it's a magical time to visit, especially during the holiday season. Christmas markets, ice skating rinks, and cozy cafés create a charming atmosphere. If you're lucky, you might even experience a picturesque snowfall.

Overall, the best time to visit the Netherlands depends on your interests and what you hope to experience during your trip. Each season has its own unique charm, so whether you're drawn to vibrant blooms, outdoor festivals, or cozy winter scenes, you're sure to find the perfect time to explore this captivating country.

Visa Requirements and Travel Documents

When planning a trip to the Netherlands, it's important to understand the visa requirements and necessary travel documents. Here's an overview to help you prepare:

- **Visa Requirements:** The visa requirements for the Netherlands depend on your nationality and the purpose and duration of your visit. The Netherlands is part of the Schengen Area, which allows visitors to travel freely across multiple European countries with a single visa. If you are a citizen of a Schengen Area country, you generally do not need a visa for short visits. However, if you are a citizen of a non-Schengen country, you may need to apply for a Schengen visa in advance. Check with the Dutch embassy or consulate in your home country to determine if you need a visa and the specific requirements for your visit.
- **Passport:** Ensure that your passport is valid for at least three months beyond your planned departure date from

the Netherlands. It's advisable to have a passport with at least two blank pages for entry and exit stamps.
- **Travel Insurance:** While travel insurance is not a mandatory requirement for entering the Netherlands, it is highly recommended. Travel insurance provides coverage for medical emergencies, trip cancellations or disruptions, and lost or stolen belongings. Make sure your policy covers the duration of your trip and offers sufficient coverage for your needs.
- **Additional Documents:** It is a good practice to carry supporting documents such as flight reservations, hotel bookings, and a detailed itinerary of your trip. These documents may be required for immigration purposes or to provide evidence of your travel plans if requested.

It's crucial to check the visa requirements well in advance of your trip and allow sufficient time for the visa application process if needed. Ensure that you have all the necessary travel documents in order to have a smooth and hassle-free entry into the Netherlands.

Health and Safety Tips

When visiting the Netherlands, it's important to prioritize your health and safety. Here are some tips to ensure a safe and enjoyable trip:

1. **Travel Insurance:** Before your trip, make sure you have comprehensive travel insurance that covers medical emergencies, trip cancellations, and lost or stolen belongings. It's essential to have adequate coverage to protect yourself in case of unforeseen circumstances.
2. **Medical Care:** The Netherlands has a high standard of medical care. If you require medical attention, look for a local general practitioner (huisarts) or visit the nearest hospital. Keep your travel insurance details and emergency contact numbers easily accessible.
3. **Vaccinations:** Check with your healthcare provider regarding recommended vaccinations for your trip to the Netherlands. Routine vaccinations, such as measles, mumps, and rubella (MMR), diphtheria-tetanus-pertussis, and influenza, are generally advised.
4. **Medications:** If you take prescription medications, ensure you have an adequate supply for the duration of

your trip. Carry them in their original packaging, along with the prescriptions or doctor's notes, to avoid any issues at customs.
5. **Safety Precautions:** The Netherlands is considered a safe country for travelers. However, it's always wise to exercise common safety precautions. Stay aware of your surroundings, particularly in crowded tourist areas, and keep your belongings secure. Avoid displaying valuables or carrying large sums of cash.
6. **Transportation Safety:** The Netherlands has a well-developed public transportation system, including trains, trams, and buses. Follow safety guidelines, such as standing behind the yellow line on train platforms and using designated pedestrian crossings. If you rent a bicycle, familiarize yourself with local cycling rules and use proper safety equipment.
7. **Weather Precautions:** The Dutch weather can be unpredictable, so pack appropriate clothing for changing conditions. Carry an umbrella or raincoat to prepare for occasional showers. During winter, be cautious of icy surfaces and wear appropriate footwear.
8. **Emergency Services:** Familiarize yourself with the local emergency contact numbers. In the Netherlands, dial 112 for any emergency, including police, fire, or medical assistance.

By following these health and safety tips, you can have a worry-free and enjoyable visit to the Netherlands. Remember to stay informed, plan ahead, and prioritize your well-being throughout your trip.

Budgeting and Money Matters

When planning a trip to the Netherlands, it's important to consider budgeting and money matters to ensure a smooth and financially sound experience. Here are some tips to help you manage your expenses:

1. **Currency:** The currency in the Netherlands is the Euro (EUR). It's advisable to carry some cash in Euros for smaller expenses and situations where cards may not be accepted.
2. **Exchange Rates:** Stay informed about the current exchange rates before exchanging your money. Compare rates from different sources to get the best value for your currency. Avoid exchanging money at airports or tourist areas, as they often offer less favorable rates.
3. **Payment Methods:** Debit and credit cards are widely accepted in the Netherlands, especially in major cities and tourist areas. Ensure that your cards are enabled for international use and notify your bank of your travel plans to prevent any issues with card transactions. Contactless payment methods, such as Apple Pay or Google Pay, are also commonly used.

4. **ATM Withdrawals:** ATMs are widely available throughout the country, and they offer a convenient way to withdraw cash. Be mindful of potential fees and foreign transaction charges that your bank may impose. Look for ATMs associated with major banks to minimize additional charges.
5. **Budget Accommodation:** Consider staying in budget-friendly accommodations, such as hostels, guesthouses, or budget hotels. Booking in advance can often provide better rates and options. Additionally, consider accommodations outside major cities for potentially lower prices.
6. **Dining Options:** Eating out in restaurants can be costly, especially in touristy areas. Consider trying local markets, food stalls, or affordable eateries for budget-friendly meals. Supermarkets and grocery stores offer a variety of fresh produce, snacks, and beverages at reasonable prices, which is ideal for self-catering or picnics.
7. **Transportation:** Public transportation, such as trains and buses, is a cost-effective way to get around the Netherlands. Consider purchasing travel passes or cards that offer unlimited travel within a specified period, as they can provide savings.
8. **Free and Low-Cost Attractions:** The Netherlands has many attractions and activities that are free or have low entrance fees. Take advantage of city parks, walking tours, and museums with discounted or free admission on certain days.

Updated Netherlands Travel Guide

By planning your budget and making informed choices, you can make the most of your funds while exploring the Netherlands. Remember to keep track of your expenses, make use of cost-saving options, and allocate your budget wisely to have a memorable and financially responsible trip.

Getting Around the Netherlands

Getting around the Netherlands is a breeze thanks to its efficient and well-connected transportation system. Here are the various options available for traveling within the country:

1. **Trains:** The Dutch railway network is extensive, providing fast and reliable connections between major cities and towns. The Nederlandse Spoorwegen (NS) operates the train services, offering comfortable and frequent trains. Consider purchasing an OV-chipkaart, a contactless smart card that allows for convenient travel on trains and other forms of public transport.
2. **Buses:** Buses are another common mode of transportation in the Netherlands, particularly for reaching smaller towns and rural areas where train connections may be limited. Both regional and national bus services are available, with reliable schedules and comfortable amenities.
3. **Trams and Metro:** Major cities like Amsterdam, Rotterdam, The Hague, and Utrecht have extensive tram and metro networks. These systems provide convenient transportation within the city, with regular service and easy-to-understand routes. Tickets for trams and metro

can be purchased at vending machines or using an OV-chipkaart.
4. **Cycling:** The Netherlands is renowned for its cycling culture and infrastructure, making it a fantastic country to explore on two wheels. Many cities offer bicycle rentals, and there are dedicated cycling paths throughout the country. Renting a bike provides an eco-friendly and leisurely way to discover the Dutch landscapes and city streets.
5. **Ferries:** The Netherlands is crisscrossed by canals, rivers, and waterways, and ferries are a common means of transportation, especially in areas like Amsterdam and Rotterdam. Ferries can take you across bodies of water or provide scenic tours, adding a unique dimension to your travel experience.
6. **Car Rentals:** While public transportation is highly efficient, renting a car gives you the flexibility to explore remote areas and the countryside at your own pace. However, keep in mind that parking can be limited and expensive in city centers.

The Netherlands' compact size and well-connected infrastructure make it easy to travel between cities and explore different regions. Plan your routes in advance, consider purchasing the appropriate travel passes or cards, and enjoy the convenience and accessibility of getting around the Netherlands.

EXPLORING AMSTERDAM

Amsterdam, the capital city of the Netherlands, is a vibrant and culturally rich destination that attracts millions of visitors each year. Known for its picturesque canals, historic architecture, and artistic heritage, Amsterdam offers a unique blend of old-world charm and modern sophistication.

The city is famous for its extensive canal system, which has earned it the nickname "Venice of the North." Exploring the canals by boat or simply strolling along their banks is a delightful way to experience the city's beauty. The UNESCO-listed Canal Ring, with its elegant canal houses and picturesque bridges, is a must-see.

Amsterdam is home to world-class museums and art galleries. The Rijksmuseum showcases Dutch masterpieces, including Rembrandt's "The Night Watch," while the Van Gogh Museum

Updated Netherlands Travel Guide

houses the largest collection of Van Gogh's works in the world. The Anne Frank House provides a poignant glimpse into the life of Anne Frank and the horrors of the Holocaust.

The city's cultural scene is vibrant, with a diverse array of theaters, music venues, and festivals. The Concertgebouw is renowned for its exceptional acoustics and hosts performances by renowned orchestras and musicians. Amsterdam's nightlife is also legendary, with a wide selection of bars, clubs, and live music venues catering to every taste.

Amsterdam embraces its reputation as a bicycle-friendly city, and cycling is a popular mode of transportation for locals and visitors alike. Renting a bike allows you to explore the city's charming neighborhoods, parks, and markets at a leisurely pace.

With its rich history, artistic treasures, charming canals, and vibrant atmosphere, Amsterdam offers a truly memorable experience for travelers seeking a mix of culture, history, and urban exploration.

Top Attractions and Landmarks

Amsterdam, the capital city of the Netherlands, is brimming with fascinating attractions and iconic landmarks that showcase its rich history and vibrant culture. Here are some of the top must-visit destinations in Amsterdam:

1. **Anne Frank House:** Step into the world of Anne Frank, the young Jewish girl who hid from the Nazis during World War II. Explore the secret annex where she wrote her famous diary, gaining insight into the wartime experience and the importance of tolerance.
2. **Rijksmuseum:** Discover the masterpieces of Dutch art and history at the Rijksmuseum. Admire works by Rembrandt, Vermeer, and other Dutch masters, including the renowned "The Night Watch." The museum's extensive collection spans centuries and offers a comprehensive overview of Dutch culture.
3. **Van Gogh Museum:** Immerse yourself in the vibrant and expressive art of Vincent van Gogh. The museum houses the largest collection of Van Gogh's works in the world, allowing visitors to trace his artistic journey and gain a deeper understanding of his life and legacy.

4. **Dam Square:** Located in the heart of Amsterdam, Dam Square is a bustling hub and a historical focal point. Admire the grand Royal Palace, which was once the city's town hall, and visit the National Monument, a tribute to the Dutch victims of World War II.
5. **Jordaan:** Explore the charming neighborhood of Jordaan, known for its picturesque streets, trendy boutiques, and cozy cafés. This historic district offers a glimpse into Amsterdam's past with its narrow canals, traditional houses, and hidden courtyards.
6. **Vondelpark:** Escape the urban hustle and bustle in the peaceful oasis of Vondelpark. This sprawling green space is ideal for picnics, leisurely walks, and cycling. Enjoy the open-air theater, ponds, and beautiful gardens that make it a favorite spot for locals and visitors alike.
7. **Canal Cruise:** Embark on a canal cruise to experience the enchanting beauty of Amsterdam's waterways. Glide along the historic canals, passing by elegant canal houses, charming bridges, and picturesque houseboats. The cruise provides a unique perspective of the city's architecture and allows you to soak in its romantic ambiance.

These top attractions and landmarks in Amsterdam offer a glimpse into the city's rich heritage, artistic treasures, and enchanting landscapes. Whether you're interested in history, art, or simply enjoying the laid-back atmosphere, Amsterdam has something to captivate every visitor.

Museums and Galleries

Amsterdam is a haven for art lovers and history enthusiasts, boasting a wealth of world-class museums and galleries that showcase an impressive array of artistic treasures and cultural artifacts. Here are some of the top museums and galleries in Amsterdam:

1. **Rijksmuseum:** The Rijksmuseum is the Netherlands' premier art museum, housing an extensive collection spanning over 800 years of Dutch art and history. It features masterpieces by Dutch masters such as Rembrandt, Vermeer, and Frans Hals. The museum's iconic "The Night Watch" by Rembrandt is a must-see.
2. **Van Gogh Museum:** Dedicated to the life and works of the legendary Dutch painter Vincent van Gogh, the Van Gogh Museum boasts the largest collection of Van Gogh's art in the world. Visitors can admire his famous paintings, including "Sunflowers," "The Bedroom," and "Starry Night," while gaining insight into his artistic evolution.
3. **Anne Frank House:** The Anne Frank House offers a poignant and moving experience, providing a glimpse into the hiding place where Anne Frank and her family

sought refuge during World War II. The museum chronicles Anne Frank's life through her diary and exhibits, shedding light on the Holocaust and the resilience of the human spirit.
4. **Stedelijk Museum:** The Stedelijk Museum is a leading contemporary art museum featuring a vast collection of modern and contemporary artworks. From abstract expressionism to pop art and beyond, the museum showcases influential artists like Mondrian, Warhol, and Kandinsky, pushing the boundaries of artistic expression.
5. **Hermitage Amsterdam:** Located in a beautiful historic building, the Hermitage Amsterdam is a branch of the famous Hermitage Museum in St. Petersburg, Russia. It presents rotating exhibitions that highlight various aspects of Russian art and culture, providing a captivating journey through history.
6. **Museum Het Rembrandthuis:** Visit the former residence of the renowned Dutch painter Rembrandt van Rijn, which has been transformed into a museum dedicated to his life and work. Explore his studio, art collection, and learn about his techniques and artistic process.
7. **NEMO Science Museum:** Perfect for families and science enthusiasts, NEMO is an interactive science museum housed in a distinctive green building shaped like a ship. It offers hands-on exhibits and activities that explore various scientific principles, making learning fun for visitors of all ages.

Amsterdam's museums and galleries offer a diverse range of artistic styles, historical narratives, and thought-provoking exhibits. From classical masterpieces to contemporary installations, there is something for everyone to explore and appreciate in this vibrant cultural hub.

Canals and Boat Tours

Amsterdam's intricate network of canals is an iconic feature of the city, earning it the nickname "Venice of the North." Exploring the canals and taking a boat tour is a quintessential Amsterdam experience that offers a unique perspective of the city's beauty and charm.

The canals, which date back to the 17th century, are a UNESCO World Heritage site and serve as a testament to Amsterdam's rich history and innovative urban planning. The three main canals, Herengracht, Prinsengracht, and Keizersgracht, form concentric rings that encircle the historic city center, lined with elegant canal houses and picturesque bridges.

Taking a boat tour allows you to admire Amsterdam's architectural gems from a different vantage point. Several tour operators offer guided cruises that provide an informative commentary, highlighting the history, landmarks, and hidden gems along the canals. You can choose from a variety of options, including open-air boats, traditional canal boats, or even luxury dinner cruises.

One of the best times to experience the canals is during the evening when the city is bathed in warm golden light. The illuminated bridges and buildings create a magical atmosphere as you glide along the water, passing by cozy waterfront cafés and charming houseboats.

Aside from organized boat tours, you can also rent a small boat or pedal boat for a more intimate and leisurely canal experience. Navigating the canals at your own pace allows you to discover quieter corners and enjoy the peaceful ambiance.

The canals also play host to various events throughout the year. One of the most famous is the annual Amsterdam Light Festival, where artists illuminate the city with captivating light installations, creating a mesmerizing spectacle along the waterways.

Whether you choose a guided boat tour or opt for independent exploration, Amsterdam's canals offer a serene and enchanting backdrop to discover the city's beauty. Soak in the picturesque views, marvel at the historic architecture, and immerse yourself in the charm of Amsterdam's waterways.

Parks and Outdoor Activities

Amsterdam is a city that seamlessly blends urban living with ample green spaces and outdoor activities. The city's parks offer a refreshing escape from the bustling streets, providing opportunities for relaxation, recreation, and exploration. Here are some of the top parks and outdoor activities in Amsterdam:

1. **Vondelpark:** Located in the heart of the city, Vondelpark is Amsterdam's most famous and beloved park. Spanning over 120 acres, it features lush lawns, picturesque ponds, winding paths, and beautiful flowerbeds. It's the perfect spot for a leisurely stroll, a picnic with friends, or even a bike ride. The park also hosts open-air theater performances during the summer months.
2. **Amsterdamse Bos:** Just outside the city center lies Amsterdamse Bos, a vast forested area with an extensive network of walking and cycling paths. This recreational park offers activities such as canoeing, horse riding, and swimming in its lakes. It's an ideal place to connect with nature, enjoy a picnic, or simply unwind amidst the greenery.

3. **Westerpark:** Located in the Westerpark neighborhood, this park is known for its relaxed atmosphere and cultural offerings. It features a mix of open spaces, water features, and recreational facilities. Westerpark also houses cultural venues like the Westergas, a former industrial complex transformed into a hub for arts, music, and dining.
4. **Hortus Botanicus:** Step into a world of natural beauty at the Hortus Botanicus, one of the oldest botanical gardens in the world. Situated in the Plantage neighborhood, this peaceful oasis is home to an extensive collection of exotic plants, trees, and flowers. Explore various climates within the garden's different sections, including tropical greenhouses and serene outdoor spaces.
5. **Biking:** Amsterdam is renowned for its cycling culture, and biking is one of the best ways to explore the city and its surroundings. Rent a bike and pedal along the designated bike paths, taking in the sights and enjoying the freedom of two wheels. You can cycle along the canals, venture into the countryside, or simply navigate the city's bike-friendly streets.
6. **Watersports:** Amsterdam's extensive network of canals and nearby lakes provides opportunities for various watersports. You can rent a boat, kayak, or paddleboard to explore the waterways or even try your hand at sailing or windsurfing.

Amsterdam's parks and outdoor activities offer a chance to connect with nature, enjoy recreational pursuits, and experience the city's outdoor lifestyle. Whether you're looking for a peaceful retreat or an active adventure, these green spaces provide the perfect backdrop for relaxation and exploration.

Shopping and Markets

Amsterdam is a shopper's paradise, offering a diverse range of shopping experiences, from trendy boutiques and high-end department stores to unique markets and vintage shops. Here are some of the top shopping destinations and markets in Amsterdam:

1. **Nine Streets (De Negen Straatjes):** Located in the heart of Amsterdam's canal district, the Nine Streets are a collection of charming streets lined with boutique shops, vintage stores, and independent designers. Here, you'll find a mix of fashion, accessories, home decor, and specialty stores, making it a haven for fashion-forward individuals and those seeking one-of-a-kind items.
2. **Kalverstraat:** As one of the busiest shopping streets in Amsterdam, Kalverstraat is home to numerous international chains, department stores, and popular fashion brands. From H&M and Zara to luxury brands like Louis Vuitton and Gucci, this bustling street caters to a wide range of shopping preferences.
3. **Albert Cuyp Market:** One of the oldest and most famous markets in Amsterdam, Albert Cuyp Market

offers a vibrant atmosphere and a wide variety of products. From fresh produce and seafood to clothing, accessories, and household goods, you can find almost anything at this bustling street market. It's an excellent place to experience the local culture, sample street food, and hunt for bargains.

4. **Waterlooplein Flea Market:** Located near the city center, Waterlooplein Flea Market is the largest flea market in Amsterdam. It offers a treasure trove of vintage clothing, antiques, books, and second-hand items. Whether you're searching for unique clothing pieces, vinyl records, or quirky collectibles, this market is a haven for vintage enthusiasts.
5. **P.C. Hooftstraat:** For those seeking luxury and high-end shopping, P.C. Hooftstraat is the place to go. This upscale shopping street is home to renowned fashion brands like Chanel, Prada, and Dior, as well as exclusive boutiques and jewelry stores. It's a destination for luxury shopping and browsing the latest designer collections.
6. **Food Markets:** Amsterdam also offers a variety of food markets where you can sample local delicacies and buy fresh produce. The Foodhallen, located in a converted tram depot, offers a wide selection of international cuisines and gourmet bites. The Noordermarkt is known for its organic products, including fresh produce, cheese, and flowers.

Dining and Nightlife

Amsterdam's dining and nightlife scene is as diverse and vibrant as the city itself, offering a plethora of options to suit every taste and preference. From traditional Dutch cuisine to international flavors and cozy pubs to trendy clubs, here's a glimpse into the dining and nightlife experiences in Amsterdam:

Dining

Amsterdam boasts a rich culinary landscape with a wide range of dining options. You can savor traditional Dutch dishes such as herring, bitterballen (deep-fried meatballs), and stroopwafels (syrup waffles) at local eateries and street food stalls.

For a more contemporary culinary experience, the city offers a plethora of international cuisines, from Italian and Asian to Middle Eastern and beyond. Amsterdam is also known for its innovative and sustainable dining scene, with many restaurants embracing farm-to-table concepts and showcasing local ingredients.

Jordaan and De Pijp neighborhoods are popular foodie destinations, featuring a mix of trendy restaurants, cozy cafés, and street food markets. The city's multicultural makeup means you can find authentic flavors from around the world, whether you're craving Moroccan tagine, Indonesian rijsttafel, or Lebanese mezze.

Nightlife

Amsterdam comes alive after dark, offering a vibrant and diverse nightlife scene. The city is known for its cozy brown cafés, where you can enjoy a wide selection of Dutch beers and traditional pub fare. These charming establishments offer a relaxed atmosphere and are perfect for socializing with friends or enjoying a laid-back evening.

For those seeking a more lively atmosphere, Amsterdam is home to numerous bars, clubs, and music venues. The Rembrandtplein and Leidseplein squares are hotspots for nightlife, offering a mix of bars, clubs, and live music venues that cater to various tastes in music and entertainment.

Amsterdam is also famous for its thriving electronic music scene, with clubs like De School, Shelter, and Paradiso hosting internationally renowned DJs and artists. The city's dance festivals, such as Amsterdam Dance Event (ADE), attract electronic music enthusiasts from around the world.

In addition to traditional nightlife, Amsterdam offers unique experiences such as canal cruises with dinner and drinks, allowing you to enjoy the city's picturesque canals while indulging in a delicious meal.

Updated Netherlands Travel Guide

Whether you're looking for a cozy pub, a trendy cocktail bar, or a night of dancing, Amsterdam's dining and nightlife scene offers a diverse array of options that will satisfy even the most discerning visitors.

Updated Netherlands Travel Guide

BEYOND AMSTERDAM: HIGHLIGHTS OF THE NETHERLANDS

While Amsterdam is undoubtedly a captivating city, there is much more to explore beyond its borders. The Netherlands is a country rich in cultural heritage, picturesque landscapes, and charming towns.

Take a day trip to the famous windmills of Kinderdijk or visit the historic city of Utrecht with its stunning canals and

Updated Netherlands Travel Guide

medieval architecture. Explore the beautiful tulip fields in Lisse during the spring or venture to the fairy-tale village of Giethoorn, known as the "Venice of the North." From the charming streets of Delft to the vibrant port city of Rotterdam, the highlights of the Netherlands extend far beyond Amsterdam.

Rotterdam

Rotterdam, the second-largest city in the Netherlands, is a vibrant and dynamic metropolis that showcases modern architecture, a thriving cultural scene, and a bustling port. Known for its innovative spirit and resilience after being heavily bombed during World War II, Rotterdam has transformed into a city that embraces contemporary design and urban development. Here's a glimpse into what makes Rotterdam a must-visit destination:

1. **Architecture:** Rotterdam is an architectural playground featuring iconic buildings that push boundaries and defy convention. The striking Erasmus Bridge, the futuristic Markthal (Market Hall), and the Cube Houses are just a few examples of the city's architectural marvels. The Rotterdam skyline is a blend of bold and imaginative structures, creating a visually captivating cityscape.
2. **Cultural Diversity:** Rotterdam is a melting pot of cultures and nationalities, reflected in its diverse culinary scene, vibrant festivals, and international events. The city hosts the International Film Festival Rotterdam, showcasing innovative cinema from around the world, and the vibrant Carnival, which celebrates multiculturalism with colorful parades and festivities.
3. **Art and Museums:** Rotterdam is home to numerous world-class museums and galleries. The Kunsthal Rotterdam offers a dynamic mix of contemporary art,

while the Museum Boijmans Van Beuningen houses an extensive collection of old masters and modern art. The Netherlands Architecture Institute (NAI) is a must-visit for architecture enthusiasts, showcasing the evolution of Dutch architecture.
4. **Port of Rotterdam:** As Europe's largest port, the Port of Rotterdam is a vital economic hub and a testament to the city's maritime heritage. Visitors can take boat tours to witness the impressive scale of the port and learn about its history and operations.
5. **Food and Drink:** Rotterdam's culinary scene is diverse and dynamic, offering a wide range of international cuisines and innovative gastronomy. From trendy food markets like Fenix Food Factory to Michelin-starred restaurants, there are options to suit every taste and budget. Don't miss the opportunity to try local specialties like bitterballen and Rotterdam's own gin, known as jenever.

Rotterdam's energy, modernity, and cultural richness make it a captivating destination for travelers seeking a vibrant city experience. With its cutting-edge architecture, cultural diversity, and thriving arts scene, Rotterdam offers a unique and refreshing perspective on the Netherlands' urban landscape.

The Hague

The Hague, known as Den Haag in Dutch, is a fascinating city that serves as the political and administrative heart of the Netherlands. It is home to the Dutch government, international organizations, and foreign embassies, making it an important global hub. Here's a glimpse into what makes The Hague a compelling destination:

1. **International Importance:** The Hague is renowned for its role in international law and diplomacy. The city houses the International Court of Justice, the principal judicial organ of the United Nations, and the International Criminal Court. Visitors can explore the Peace Palace, an architectural gem that symbolizes The Hague's commitment to peace and justice.
2. **Cultural and Historical Heritage:** The Hague boasts a rich cultural and historical heritage. The Mauritshuis Museum is a must-visit, housing iconic masterpieces like Vermeer's "Girl with a Pearl Earring" and Rembrandt's "The Anatomy Lesson of Dr. Nicolaes Tulp." The Binnenhof, a medieval complex of buildings, is the center of Dutch politics and offers a glimpse into the country's history.
3. **Beaches and Nature:** The Hague is uniquely situated on the coast of the North Sea, offering beautiful sandy beaches that are popular with locals and tourists alike. Scheveningen, the city's most famous seaside resort,

features a long promenade, beach clubs, and a lively atmosphere. The nearby Westduinpark and Meijendel nature reserves provide opportunities for hiking, biking, and exploring nature trails.
4. **Cultural Scene:** The Hague is a cultural hub with a vibrant arts and music scene. The city is home to numerous theaters, music venues, and art galleries. The Zuiderstrandtheater and Koninklijke Schouwburg showcase a variety of performances, including theater, dance, and music. The annual Crossing Border Festival attracts renowned writers, poets, and musicians from around the world.
5. **Shopping and Dining:** The Hague offers a diverse range of shopping experiences, from high-end boutiques to local markets. The Passage, a historic shopping arcade, is a favorite among shoppers. The city also boasts an array of dining options, with a mix of international cuisines and Dutch specialties. The trendy Hofkwartier neighborhood is a popular spot for boutique shopping and culinary delights.

The Hague's blend of international significance, cultural heritage, and natural beauty makes it a captivating destination. Whether you're interested in history, art, politics, or simply enjoying the beach, The Hague offers a unique and enriching experience in the heart of the Netherlands.

Utrecht

Utrecht, located in the heart of the Netherlands, is a vibrant city with a rich history, charming canals, and a lively cultural scene. Here's an overview of what makes Utrecht a captivating destination:

1. **Historic Beauty:** Utrecht is one of the oldest cities in the Netherlands, dating back to Roman times. Its historic center is characterized by picturesque canals, narrow streets, and beautifully preserved medieval buildings. The iconic Dom Tower, the tallest church tower in the country, offers stunning panoramic views of the city.
2. **University City:** Utrecht is home to one of the largest and oldest universities in the Netherlands, giving the city a youthful and energetic atmosphere. The vibrant student population contributes to the city's dynamic arts, music, and nightlife scenes. The cultural offerings are diverse and include theaters, concert halls, and art galleries.
3. **Canal Cruises:** Utrecht's canals, known as "grachten," is a defining feature of the city. Taking a canal cruise allows visitors to admire the historical architecture and enjoy a unique perspective of Utrecht. The canals are lined with cafes, restaurants, and shops, creating a delightful ambiance.
4. **Cultural Highlights:** Utrecht offers a range of cultural attractions. The Centraal Museum houses an extensive

collection of art, including works by Dutch masters such as Rietveld and Van Doesburg. The Museum Speelklok celebrates the history of self-playing musical instruments. For music lovers, TivoliVredenburg is a renowned music venue that hosts a variety of concerts and performances.
5. **Parks and Gardens:** Utrecht is known for its green spaces and outdoor areas. The Griftpark is a popular spot for picnics and recreational activities, while the Botanic Gardens provide a tranquil escape with beautiful plant collections. The Máximapark, one of the largest parks in the Netherlands, offers vast green landscapes, playgrounds, and walking and cycling paths.
6. **Culinary Delights:** Utrecht has a thriving food and drink scene. The city is dotted with cozy cafes, trendy restaurants, and traditional Dutch pubs. Visitors can savor local specialties such as "stroopwafels" (syrup waffles) and "Oudegrachtse Sprits" (butter biscuits).

Utrecht's combination of historical charm, cultural vibrancy, and natural beauty make it a captivating destination in the Netherlands. Whether you're exploring its canals, immersing yourself in its cultural offerings, or simply enjoying the laid-back atmosphere, Utrecht offers a memorable and enriching experience.

Maastricht

Maastricht, located in the southernmost part of the Netherlands, is a charming city with a rich history, a blend of cultural influences, and a vibrant atmosphere. Here's an overview of what makes Maastricht a captivating destination:

1. **Historical Significance**: Maastricht is one of the oldest cities in the Netherlands, dating back to Roman times. Its historical heritage is evident in its architecture, with highlights such as the Basilica of Saint Servatius and the Helpoort, the oldest surviving city gate in the Netherlands. The city's winding streets and squares are lined with beautifully preserved buildings, creating a picturesque setting.
2. **Cultural Melting Pot:** Due to its strategic location close to the borders of Belgium and Germany, Maastricht has been influenced by various cultures throughout its history. This is reflected in its unique blend of Dutch, French, and German influences. The city is known for its cosmopolitan vibe, with a diverse culinary scene, international festivals, and a thriving arts and music scene.
3. **Shopping and Dining:** Maastricht offers a delightful shopping experience with its mix of high-end fashion boutiques, unique concept stores, and artisanal shops. Stroll along the charming streets of the historic city center, such as Stokstraatkwartier and Wyck, to discover

hidden gems. Maastricht is also renowned for its culinary scene, with a wide range of restaurants, cafes, and brasseries offering both local and international cuisine.
4. **Vrijthof Square:** The Vrijthof is Maastricht's central square and a popular gathering place for locals and visitors alike. It is surrounded by historic buildings, including the imposing Saint Servatius Basilica and the Saint John's Church. The square hosts various events and concerts throughout the year, including the André Rieu concerts, which draw thousands of music lovers from around the world.
5. **Nature and Surroundings:** Maastricht is surrounded by beautiful countryside and is a gateway to exploring the picturesque Limburg region. The nearby St. Pietersberg Hill offers hiking trails and panoramic views of the city and the Maas River. The region is also known for its vineyards, cycling routes, and the scenic Maas Valley.

Maastricht's blend of history, culture, shopping, and natural beauty makes it a captivating destination in the Netherlands. Whether you're exploring its historical sites, indulging in its culinary delights, or immersing yourself in its vibrant atmosphere, Maastricht offers a memorable and enchanting experience.

Groningen

Groningen, located in the northern part of the Netherlands, is a vibrant and charming city known for its rich history, thriving cultural scene, and lively student population. Here's an overview of what makes Groningen a captivating destination:

1. **Historical and Architectural Beauty:** Groningen is a city steeped in history, with a well-preserved medieval center. The iconic Martinitoren, a towering church tower, dominates the skyline and offers panoramic views of the city. The Grote Markt, the central square, is surrounded by historic buildings and bustling cafes. The Aa-Kerk and the Prinsentuin, a beautiful Renaissance-style garden, are also must-visit attractions.
2. **Student City:** Groningen is home to one of the oldest and largest universities in the Netherlands, attracting a vibrant student population. The presence of students adds to the city's youthful and dynamic atmosphere. The student influence can be felt throughout the city, with lively bars, cafes, and cultural events.
3. **Cultural Offerings:** Groningen has a thriving cultural scene with a variety of museums, theaters, and art galleries. The Groninger Museum, designed by renowned architect Alessandro Mendini, is a striking building housing an impressive collection of modern and contemporary art. The Noorderlicht Photography

Gallery and the Groninger Forum are also popular venues for art and cultural exhibitions.
4. **Biking Culture:** Like much of the Netherlands, Groningen is known for its cycling culture. The city boasts excellent bike infrastructure, making it easy to explore on two wheels. Rent a bike and discover the city's beautiful parks, canals, and historic neighborhoods.
5. **Festivals and Events:** Groningen hosts a wide range of festivals and events throughout the year. The Eurosonic Noorderslag music festival, showcasing emerging European artists, attracts music enthusiasts from around the world. The Noorderzon Performing Arts Festival and the Groningen Museum Night are other highlights that showcase the city's vibrant cultural scene.
6. **Green Spaces:** Groningen offers plenty of green spaces for relaxation and recreation. The Noorderplantsoen, a beautiful park with scenic paths and a lake, is a popular spot for picnics and outdoor activities. The city's canals, such as the Hoge and Lage Der A, offer tranquil settings for leisurely walks.

Groningen's mix of history, culture, and youthful energy make it a captivating destination in the Netherlands. Whether you're exploring its historical sites, immersing yourself in its cultural offerings, or simply enjoying the lively atmosphere, Groningen offers a unique and memorable experience.

Updated Netherlands Travel Guide

Updated Netherlands Travel Guide

Haarlem

Haarlem, located just a short distance from Amsterdam, is a picturesque city in the Netherlands with a rich history, stunning architecture, and a thriving cultural scene. Here's an overview of what makes Haarlem a captivating destination:

1. **Historical Significance:** Haarlem boasts a fascinating history that dates back to the Middle Ages. The city's historic center is filled with beautifully preserved buildings, cobblestone streets, and charming canals. The Grote Markt, the central square, is the heart of Haarlem and is surrounded by notable landmarks such as the magnificent St. Bavo's Church and the City Hall.
2. **Artistic Heritage:** Haarlem has long been associated with art and has been a source of inspiration for many famous painters. The Frans Hals Museum showcases the works of the renowned Dutch Golden Age painter, Frans Hals, as well as other masters of the era. The Teylers Museum, the oldest museum in the Netherlands, houses a diverse collection of art, science, and natural history.
3. **Gardens and Parks:** Haarlem is known for its beautiful gardens and green spaces. The Haarlemmerhout Park, one of the oldest public parks in the Netherlands, offers serene walking paths, open fields, and a charming teahouse. The nearby Keukenhof Gardens, famous for their vibrant displays of tulips and other spring flowers,

are a short distance from Haarlem and attract visitors from around the world.
4. **Shopping and Dining:** Haarlem offers a delightful shopping experience with its mix of boutiques, specialty stores, and artisanal shops. The city's main shopping streets, such as Grote Houtstraat and Kleine Houtstraat, are lined with unique shops selling fashion, design, and local products. Haarlem is also home to a variety of restaurants, cafes, and bars where visitors can enjoy both local and international cuisines.
5. **Festivals and Events:** Haarlem hosts several festivals and events throughout the year that showcase its lively cultural scene. The Haarlem Jazz & More Festival attracts renowned musicians from various genres, while the Haarlemse Stripdagen celebrates comics and graphic novels. The annual Bloemencorso, or Flower Parade, features elaborately decorated floats adorned with colorful blooms.

Haarlem's blend of history, art, natural beauty, and cultural vibrancy make it a captivating destination. Whether you're exploring its historic sites, immersing yourself in its artistic heritage, or simply enjoying the relaxed ambiance, Haarlem offers a memorable and enriching experience.

Delft

Delft, a small and charming city in the Netherlands, is renowned for its rich history, beautiful canals, and distinctive blue and white pottery. Here's an overview of what makes Delft a captivating destination:

1. **Historical Significance:** Delft has a fascinating history that dates back to the 13th century. The city was once a prosperous center of trade and culture and played a crucial role in the Dutch Golden Age. Delft's historic center is characterized by picturesque canals, narrow streets, and well-preserved buildings. The Markt Square is a focal point of the city, with the impressive City Hall and the towering Nieuwe Kerk (New Church) that houses the tombs of members of the Dutch royal family.
2. **Delftware and Pottery:** Delft is famous for its traditional blue and white pottery, known as Delftware. Visitors can explore the Royal Delft factory, where they can witness the intricate process of creating these beautiful hand-painted ceramics. The museum showcases a vast collection of Delftware, providing insights into its history and artistic significance.
3. **Vermeer and Dutch Masters:** Delft was the birthplace of the renowned Dutch painter Johannes Vermeer, known for his exquisite use of light and depiction of domestic scenes. The Vermeer Centrum Delft offers a glimpse into Vermeer's life and art, with reproductions

of his paintings and insights into his techniques. Additionally, Delft is in close proximity to The Hague, where art enthusiasts can visit the Mauritshuis Museum to admire Vermeer's original masterpiece, "Girl with a Pearl Earring," among other Dutch masterpieces.
4. **Canal Cruises and Waterside Charm:** Delft's canals add to its charm and provide a delightful setting for a leisurely boat ride. Exploring the city from the water allows visitors to appreciate its architectural beauty and serene atmosphere. The canal-lined streets are also home to cozy cafes, restaurants, and boutiques, creating a delightful ambiance.
5. **Technical University:** Delft is home to the Delft University of Technology, one of the leading technical universities in the world. The presence of the university contributes to a vibrant and innovative atmosphere with a diverse community of students and researchers.

Delft's blend of history, art, pottery, and waterside charm makes it a captivating destination in the Netherlands. Whether you're immersing yourself in its artistic heritage, enjoying a canal cruise, or exploring its historic sites, Delft offers a unique and memorable experience.

Updated Netherlands Travel Guide

Leiden

Leiden, located in the western Netherlands, is a historic and culturally rich city known for its prestigious university, charming canals, and significant contributions to art, science, and history. Here's an overview of what makes Leiden a captivating destination:

1. **Historical Significance:** Leiden has a long and storied history, dating back to Roman times. It played a pivotal role in the Dutch Golden Age and was the birthplace of the famous painter Rembrandt van Rijn. The city's historic center is characterized by beautiful canals, quaint bridges, and well-preserved buildings. The Burcht van Leiden, a medieval fortress, offers panoramic views of the city.
2. **Leiden University:** Leiden is home to one of the oldest and most prestigious universities in the Netherlands, Leiden University. Established in 1575, the university has been a center of learning and scholarship for centuries. Visitors can explore the university's historic buildings, including the Academiegebouw, and visit the Hortus Botanicus, one of the oldest botanical gardens in the world.
3. **Cultural and Artistic Heritage:** Leiden has a vibrant cultural scene with numerous museums, galleries, and theaters. The Museum De Lakenhal showcases art, history, and culture, including works by Rembrandt and

Updated Netherlands Travel Guide

other Dutch masters. The National Museum of Antiquities houses an impressive collection of ancient artifacts. The city's rich cultural heritage is also celebrated during the Leiden International Film Festival and the Leiden Jazz Festival.

4. **Canals and Bridges:** Leiden's canals, known as "grachten," are an integral part of the city's charm. Taking a boat tour or strolling along the canals allows visitors to admire the picturesque scenery, historic buildings, and graceful bridges. The Rapenburg Canal, in particular, is lined with beautiful 17th-century canal houses, creating a postcard-perfect scene.

5. **Parks and Gardens:** Leiden offers several parks and green spaces where visitors can relax and enjoy nature. The Van der Werfpark, located in the city center, is a tranquil park with walking paths and a peaceful atmosphere. The Hortus Botanicus, affiliated with the university, is a botanical garden that showcases a wide variety of plant species.

Leiden's blend of history, cultural heritage, and natural beauty make it a captivating destination in the Netherlands. Whether you're exploring its museums and historic sites, strolling along its canals, or immersing yourself in its academic and artistic atmosphere, Leiden offers a memorable and enriching experience.

DUTCH CULTURE AND TRADITIONS

Dutch culture and traditions are rich and diverse, shaped by the country's history, geographical location, and the values of its people. The Netherlands, known for its windmills, tulips, and canals, offers a unique cultural experience that is both intriguing and welcoming. Here's a brief introduction to Dutch culture and traditions:

1. **Tolerance and Open-mindedness:** Dutch society is known for its emphasis on tolerance and open-mindedness. The Netherlands has a long-standing

tradition of promoting equality, individual freedom, and acceptance of diversity. This inclusive mindset can be observed in the country's liberal policies, such as same-sex marriage, legalized cannabis, and an open attitude towards different lifestyles.
2. **Cycling Culture:** The Netherlands is famous for its cycling culture. Bicycles are a popular mode of transportation, and the country boasts an extensive network of cycling paths. Cycling is not just a means of getting around; it is deeply ingrained in Dutch culture as a way of staying healthy, reducing traffic congestion, and enjoying the scenic beauty of the country.
3. **Festivals and Celebrations:** The Dutch love to celebrate and have a vibrant festival culture. From King's Day (Koningsdag) in April, when the entire country dresses in orange to celebrate the king's birthday, to Sinterklaas in December, a festive tradition featuring the arrival of Saint Nicholas and gift-giving, there are numerous cultural events and celebrations throughout the year that showcase the Dutch spirit and sense of community.
4. **Cheese and Cuisine:** The Dutch take pride in their delicious cheeses, with Gouda and Edam being among the most famous varieties. Dutch cuisine is also known for its hearty comfort foods such as stamppot (mashed potatoes with vegetables) and bitterballen (deep-fried meatballs). The country's proximity to the sea means that seafood, particularly herring, plays an important role in the culinary scene.
5. **Art and Design:** The Netherlands has a rich artistic tradition, with famous Dutch masters such as Rembrandt

and Vermeer leaving an indelible mark on the world of art. Dutch design is highly regarded and known for its simplicity, functionality, and innovation. The country's museums and galleries, such as the Rijksmuseum and the Van Gogh Museum in Amsterdam, are home to world-class collections that attract art enthusiasts from around the globe.

Dutch culture and traditions are a fascinating blend of history, openness, creativity, and a love for nature. Whether you're exploring the country's museums, participating in festive celebrations, or simply enjoying a leisurely bike ride, the Dutch way of life is sure to leave a lasting impression.

History of the Netherlands

The history of the Netherlands is a tapestry woven with tales of exploration, trade, cultural exchange, and political struggles. From its humble beginnings as a collection of small feudal states to its rise as a global maritime power, the Netherlands has played a significant role in shaping European history. Here's a brief overview of the history of the Netherlands:

1. **Medieval Origins:** The region that now comprises the Netherlands has a long history dating back to the Roman era. In the Middle Ages, the area was divided into numerous independent territories ruled by local lords. The emergence of important cities like Amsterdam, Rotterdam, and Utrecht laid the foundation for future prosperity.
2. **The Dutch Golden Age:** The 17th century is often referred to as the Dutch Golden Age, a period of great economic, cultural, and scientific achievements for the Netherlands. The Dutch East India Company (VOC) dominated global trade routes, establishing colonies and amassing wealth. Dutch painters like Rembrandt and Vermeer produced masterpieces, and scholars like Hugo

Grotius made significant contributions to philosophy and law.
3. **The Dutch Republic:** In the late 16th century, the Dutch revolted against Spanish rule, leading to the establishment of the Dutch Republic in 1588. The Republic became a haven for religious refugees and emerged as a prosperous and influential European power. It championed religious tolerance, became a center for art and science, and developed a strong navy to protect its trade interests.
4. **Napoleonic Era and Kingdom of the Netherlands:** In the late 18th and early 19th centuries, the French Revolutionary and Napoleonic wars had a profound impact on the Netherlands. The French occupation led to the formation of the Kingdom of Holland, which later became part of the French Empire. After Napoleon's defeat, the Congress of Vienna in 1815 created the United Kingdom of the Netherlands, which encompassed Belgium and Luxembourg.
5. **Modern Developments:** The 19th and 20th centuries witnessed significant social, political, and economic transformations in the Netherlands. The country underwent industrialization, expanded its colonial empire, and played a pivotal role in both World Wars. After World War II, the Netherlands became a founding member of the European Union and embraced social and cultural progressivism.

Today, the Netherlands is renowned for its thriving economy, progressive social policies, and cultural contributions. Its

Updated Netherlands Travel Guide

history has shaped its identity as a nation known for its entrepreneurship, tolerance, and innovation.

Dutch Art and Architecture

Dutch art and architecture have left an indelible mark on the world, characterized by their distinctive styles, innovative techniques, and profound influence on artistic movements. From the Golden Age masterpieces of renowned painters to the unique architectural designs, Dutch art and architecture have shaped the cultural landscape of the Netherlands. Here's an overview of Dutch art and architecture:

1. **Dutch Masters**

The Netherlands is renowned for its Dutch Masters, a group of painters who emerged during the Dutch Golden Age in the 17th century. Artists such as Rembrandt van Rijn, Johannes Vermeer, and Frans Hals created timeless masterpieces that showcased their exceptional talent, mastery of light, and attention to detail. Their works often depicted everyday life, landscapes, portraits, and still lifes, capturing the essence of the Dutch spirit.

2. **Baroque and Golden Age Architecture**

The Dutch Golden Age also witnessed remarkable architectural developments. The architecture of this period was characterized by grandeur, elegance, and attention to symmetry. Amsterdam's Canal Belt, a UNESCO World Heritage site, exemplifies the unique urban planning and architectural style of the time. The canal houses, with their narrow facades, tall windows, and ornate gables, are iconic symbols of Dutch architecture.

3. **Modern and Contemporary Architecture**

The Netherlands is at the forefront of modern and contemporary architectural design. The country has produced renowned architects such as Rem Koolhaas, Piet Blom, and MVRDV. Notable examples of modern Dutch architecture include the Cube Houses in Rotterdam, the Eye Film Institute in Amsterdam, and the Ziggo Dome in Amsterdam. Innovative designs often prioritize sustainability, functionality, and integration with the surrounding environment.

4. **De Stijl Movement**

The Netherlands played a pivotal role in the development of the influential De Stijl movement. Led by artists such as Piet Mondrian and Theo van Doesburg, De Stijl sought to create a universal visual language based on simple geometric forms and primary colors. This abstract and minimalist approach had a profound impact on art, design, and architecture worldwide.

The rich legacy of Dutch art and architecture continues to inspire and captivate audiences today. The masterpieces of the Dutch Masters and the innovative designs of modern architects showcase the creativity, craftsmanship, and progressive thinking that have defined Dutch artistic expression throughout history.

Updated Netherlands Travel Guide

Festivals and Events

The Netherlands is a country known for its vibrant and diverse festival culture, with a calendar filled with lively events that celebrate everything from music and art to cultural traditions and seasonal festivities. These festivals and events offer a unique glimpse into Dutch culture, attracting both locals and visitors from around the world. Here's a glimpse into the festival and event scene in the Netherlands:

1. **King's Day (Koningsdag):** One of the biggest and most popular events in the Netherlands, King's Day is celebrated on April 27th, the birthday of King Willem-Alexander. The entire country comes alive with orange-themed festivities, including street parties, music performances, flea markets, and boat parades. It's a day when people embrace the Dutch spirit of togetherness and celebration.
2. **Carnival:** In the southern part of the Netherlands, Carnival takes center stage in the days leading up to Lent. This colorful and festive event features parades, elaborate costumes, music, and dancing. Each region puts its own unique twist on Carnival, creating a lively and joyful atmosphere.
3. **Amsterdam Dance Event (ADE):** ADE is one of the largest electronic music festivals and conferences in the world. Held in Amsterdam, it attracts renowned DJs, producers, and electronic music enthusiasts for a week

of parties, workshops, panels, and networking events. ADE showcases the vibrant electronic music scene and contributes to the city's reputation as a global hub for electronic music.
4. **Rotterdam International Film Festival (IFFR):** As one of the leading film festivals in Europe, IFFR showcases a diverse selection of independent, innovative, and thought-provoking films. It features premieres, screenings, Q&A sessions with filmmakers, and special events. The festival attracts film lovers and industry professionals from around the globe.
5. **Sinterklaas:** Celebrated on December 5th, Sinterklaas is a traditional Dutch holiday that involves the arrival of Saint Nicholas and gift-giving. The festivities include parades, Sinterklaas-themed treats, and the exchange of gifts among family and friends.

These are just a few examples of the many festivals and events that take place throughout the year in the Netherlands. Whether you're interested in music, art, cultural traditions, or seasonal celebrations, there's always something exciting happening in the vibrant festival scene of the Netherlands.

Cuisine and Local Delicacies

Dutch cuisine is a reflection of the Netherlands' rich cultural history and its relationship with the sea, agriculture, and trade. The country's culinary offerings are diverse, flavorful, and influenced by both traditional and modern influences. Here's a glimpse into the cuisine and local delicacies of the Netherlands:

1. **Cheese:** The Netherlands is famous for its cheese, and Dutch cheeses like Gouda, Edam, and Leiden are renowned worldwide. Cheese markets, such as the one in Alkmaar, showcase the craftsmanship and variety of Dutch cheeses. Visitors can sample a range of flavors and textures, from mild and creamy to aged and tangy.
2. **Herring:** Herring holds a special place in Dutch cuisine and culture. Raw herring, known as "haring," is a popular street food. It is typically served with onions and eaten by holding the fish by the tail and taking a bite. Herring is a staple at festivals and is associated with a sense of national pride.
3. **Stroopwafels:** These delightful treats consist of two thin waffle cookies with a caramel-like syrup filling in between. Stroopwafels are enjoyed as a snack or dessert, and they pair perfectly with a cup of coffee or tea. They

can be found in street markets, bakeries, and supermarkets throughout the Netherlands.
4. **Bitterballen:** Bitterballen are small, deep-fried meatballs typically filled with a mixture of beef or veal ragout. They are crispy on the outside and soft and flavorful on the inside. Bitterballen is often served as a snack with mustard and is a popular item at Dutch bars and cafes.
5. **Dutch Pancakes (Pannenkoeken):** Dutch pancakes are larger and thinner than traditional American pancakes. They can be savory or sweet and are often topped with ingredients such as bacon, cheese, apples, or powdered sugar. Pannenkoeken houses specialize in serving a variety of delicious pancake creations.

Dutch cuisine also includes dishes like erwtensoep (pea soup), stamppot (mashed potatoes mixed with vegetables), and Dutch apple pie. The Netherlands' coastal location ensures an abundance of fresh seafood, including mussels, herring, and smoked eel. Additionally, the country has embraced international flavors, with diverse restaurants offering cuisines from around the world.

Exploring Dutch cuisine and local delicacies is a delightful way to experience the country's culinary traditions and cultural heritage. From savory snacks to sweet treats, the Netherlands offers a range of flavors and dishes that are sure to tantalize the taste buds of locals and visitors alike.

Language and Etiquette

The official language of the Netherlands is Dutch, and it plays a significant role in the country's culture and daily life. Understanding a few key aspects of the Dutch language and etiquette can enhance your experience when interacting with locals. Here are some points to keep in mind:

1. **Language:** While English is widely spoken in the Netherlands, learning a few basic Dutch phrases can be helpful and appreciated. Common greetings such as "hallo" (hello) and "bedankt" (thank you) are always a good start. Locals may switch to English if they notice you struggling with Dutch, but making an effort to use the local language is often appreciated.
2. **Direct Communication:** Dutch people are known for their directness and honesty in communication. They value open and straightforward conversations, so don't be surprised if they speak their minds without much hesitation. It's important to be respectful and not take their directness personally.
3. **Punctuality:** Punctuality is highly valued in Dutch culture. Being on time for appointments, meetings, or social gatherings is considered respectful. If you're

running late, it's polite to notify the person or party you're meeting.
4. **Etiquette:** When greeting someone, a firm handshake is customary. It is also common to make eye contact during conversations as a sign of attentiveness and respect. In formal situations, it is appropriate to address people using their title and last name until you are invited to use their first name.
5. **Table Manners:** When dining in a formal setting, it is polite to wait for the host or hostess to say "eet smakelijk" (enjoy your meal) before you start eating. It is also customary to keep your hands on the table but elbows off. After finishing a meal, it is polite to place your knife and fork parallel on your plate.

Respecting personal space, being polite, and showing appreciation for the local customs and traditions will go a long way in your interactions with the Dutch people. Embracing their direct communication style and observing their etiquette will help you establish positive connections and make your experience in the Netherlands more enjoyable.

Updated Netherlands Travel Guide

OUTDOOR ADVENTURES

The Netherlands may be known for its flat landscapes and picturesque canals, but it also offers a wide range of exciting outdoor adventures. From coastal activities to countryside explorations, the Netherlands has something for every outdoor enthusiast.

Whether you're seeking thrilling water sports, peaceful hiking trails, or cycling adventures through tulip fields, this small yet diverse country has it all. Get ready to immerse yourself in the beauty of nature, breathe in the fresh air, and embark on unforgettable outdoor adventures in the Netherlands.

Updated Netherlands Travel Guide

Cycling in the Netherlands

Cycling is an integral part of Dutch culture, and the Netherlands is renowned as one of the world's most bike-friendly countries. With an extensive network of well-maintained cycling paths, flat terrain, and a strong cycling infrastructure, it's no wonder that cycling is a popular mode of transportation and a favorite pastime for both locals and visitors. Here's why cycling in the Netherlands is a must-do experience:

1. **Infrastructure:** The Netherlands boasts an impressive cycling infrastructure, with dedicated cycling paths that crisscross the country. These paths are often separate from motor vehicle traffic, ensuring a safe and enjoyable cycling experience. You'll find well-marked routes, traffic lights, and signage specifically designed for cyclists.
2. **Scenic Routes:** Cycling in the Netherlands allows you to explore the picturesque countryside, charming villages, and scenic coastal areas. You can pedal through expansive tulip fields in spring, along winding canals and past windmills that dot the landscape. The diverse scenery makes every cycling adventure a visual delight.

3. **Bike Rental and Accessibility:** Renting a bike is easy and convenient in the Netherlands. Many cities and towns have numerous rental shops where you can choose from a variety of bikes, including traditional bicycles, electric bikes, and even tandems. With bike-friendly infrastructure and accessible rental options, you can easily hop on a bike and start exploring.
4. **Cycling Culture:** The Netherlands has a strong cycling culture, with an emphasis on sustainable and active transportation. Cyclists have the right of way in many areas, and drivers are generally respectful and aware of cyclists on the road. The country's commitment to cycling as a mode of transport is evident in the countless bike racks, bike-friendly public transportation, and cycling events throughout the year.

Whether you're a casual rider or a cycling enthusiast, exploring the Netherlands on two wheels is an incredible way to immerse yourself in the local culture, appreciate the beautiful landscapes, and enjoy the freedom and convenience of cycling in one of the world's most bike-friendly countries.

Updated Netherlands Travel Guide

Hiking and Nature Reserves

While the Netherlands is known for its flat landscapes, it still offers a surprising array of hiking opportunities and stunning nature reserves. From coastal dunes to forested areas and heathlands, nature lovers will find plenty to explore. Here's a glimpse into hiking and nature reserves in the Netherlands:

1. **Nature Reserves:** The country is home to numerous nature reserves that showcase its diverse flora and fauna. The Hoge Veluwe National Park, one of the largest nature reserves in the Netherlands, boasts vast heathlands, woodlands, and sand dunes. The Biesbosch National Park, with its network of rivers, creeks, and wetlands, offers a unique and vibrant ecosystem to discover. Other notable reserves include the Drents-Friese Wold, De Meinweg, and De Weerribben-Wieden.
2. **Hiking Trails:** Despite its relatively small size, the Netherlands features an extensive network of hiking trails that cater to all skill levels. The long-distance Pieterpad trail, spanning from the northern to the southern parts of the country, takes hikers through diverse landscapes. The Veluwezoom National Park offers a variety of hiking trails amidst its forests and

heathlands. The North Holland Dune Reserve allows for scenic coastal hikes along sandy beaches and dunes.
3. **Coastal Hiking:** The Netherlands boasts a stunning coastline that offers unique opportunities for coastal hiking. The Wadden Sea, a UNESCO World Heritage site, offers breathtaking views, tidal flats, and birdwatching opportunities. The Zeeland region features beautiful coastal dunes and the Delta Works, a marvel of engineering designed to protect against flooding.
4. **Hiking Events:** The Netherlands hosts various hiking events throughout the year. The Nijmegen Four Days Marches is a renowned international walking event that attracts thousands of participants. It offers a range of distances and routes, showcasing different parts of the country. The Sallandse Heuvelrug National Park organizes the SallandTrail, a trail running event that also welcomes hikers.

Hiking in the Netherlands provides an opportunity to connect with nature, discover diverse landscapes, and appreciate the country's natural beauty. With well-marked trails, nature reserves to explore, and organized hiking events, there's something for every outdoor enthusiast to enjoy.

Water Sports and Beaches

The Netherlands is a water lover's paradise, with its extensive coastline, picturesque beaches, and numerous opportunities for water sports. From surfing and sailing to kiteboarding and canoeing, there are plenty of exciting activities to enjoy. Here's a glimpse into water sports and beaches in the Netherlands:

1. **Beaches:** The Dutch coastline stretches for miles, offering a range of beautiful sandy beaches where you can relax, sunbathe, and take in the fresh sea air. Popular beach destinations include Scheveningen, Zandvoort, and Texel, among others. Many beaches have beach clubs, restaurants, and amenities to enhance your beach experience.
2. **Surfing:** The Netherlands may not be the first place that comes to mind for surfing, but the coastal conditions make it a great destination for surf enthusiasts. Scheveningen is particularly renowned for its waves, attracting surfers of all levels. The North Sea provides consistent swells, and several surf schools offer lessons for beginners.
3. **Sailing:** With its extensive network of rivers, lakes, and canals, the Netherlands offers excellent opportunities for

sailing. The Frisian Lakes in the northern part of the country are a popular sailing destination, with pristine waters and picturesque landscapes. The IJsselmeer, once a sea but now a lake, is another sailing hotspot.
4. **Kiteboarding:** The flat and windy nature of the Netherlands makes it an ideal destination for kiteboarding. Spots like the Zandmotor near The Hague and the Brouwersdam attract kiteboarders from around the world. Lessons and equipment rentals are available for beginners and experienced riders.
5. **Canoeing and Kayaking:** The Netherlands has an extensive network of waterways, including canals, rivers, and lakes, making it perfect for canoeing and kayaking. You can explore the tranquil canals of Amsterdam, paddle through the beautiful Dutch countryside, or navigate the picturesque waterways of the Weerribben-Wieden National Park.

Water sports enthusiasts will find a host of exciting activities to indulge in along the Dutch coastline and waterways. Whether you're looking for adrenaline-pumping adventures or a more relaxed day by the beach, the Netherlands has something to offer for every water sports enthusiast.

Updated Netherlands Travel Guide

National Parks and Gardens

The Netherlands may be a relatively small country, but it is home to a surprising number of beautiful national parks and gardens that showcase its natural and horticultural wonders. From expansive heathlands to meticulously designed gardens, these parks offer a retreat into nature and a chance to explore the country's diverse landscapes. Here are some noteworthy national parks and gardens in the Netherlands:

1. **Hoge Veluwe National Park:** Located in the province of Gelderland, Hoge Veluwe National Park is one of the largest nature reserves in the country. It encompasses vast heathlands, sand dunes, woodlands, and diverse wildlife. The park is also home to the Kröller-Müller Museum, which houses an impressive collection of art, including works by Van Gogh.
2. **De Biesbosch National Park:** Situated in the province of South Holland, De Biesbosch National Park is a unique wetland area known for its network of rivers, creeks, and islands. It is a haven for birds and offers opportunities for boating, kayaking, and birdwatching. The park is also home to beavers, which can sometimes be spotted along the waterways.

3. **Keukenhof Gardens:** Keukenhof Gardens, located in Lisse, is a world-renowned floral park that celebrates the beauty of spring. It is famous for its stunning displays of tulips, daffodils, hyacinths, and other spring flowers. Millions of visitors flock to Keukenhof each year to admire the vibrant colors and intricate flower arrangements.
4. **Veluwezoom National Park:** Situated in the province of Gelderland, Veluwezoom National Park is known for its diverse landscapes, including forests, heathlands, and sand drifts. It offers picturesque hiking and cycling trails, as well as opportunities for wildlife spotting.
5. **Kroller-Muller Museum and Sculpture Park:** Located in Hoge Veluwe National Park, the Kroller-Muller Museum features an extensive collection of modern art, including works by Van Gogh and Mondrian. The museum is surrounded by a sculpture park, where visitors can enjoy art in a beautiful natural setting.

These national parks and gardens provide a sanctuary for nature lovers and a chance to appreciate the natural and artistic beauty of the Netherlands. Whether you're exploring the vast landscapes of Hoge Veluwe, marveling at the vibrant blooms of Keukenhof, or immersing yourself in the tranquility of De Biesbosch, these parks offer a delightful escape into the country's natural treasures.

Updated Netherlands Travel Guide

PRACTICAL INFORMATION

When planning a trip to the Netherlands, it's essential to have some practical information to make your visit smooth and enjoyable. This section covers important details such as currency, time zone, electrical outlets, and communication networks.

You'll also find useful information about transportation options, including public transportation and driving in the Netherlands. Additionally, we provide tips on safety, healthcare, and emergency services. Understanding these practical aspects will help you navigate the country with ease, ensuring a hassle-free and memorable experience during your time in the Netherlands.

Updated Netherlands Travel Guide

Accommodation

Options

The Netherlands offers a wide range of accommodation options to suit every traveler's preferences and budget. Whether you're looking for luxury hotels, budget-friendly hostels, cozy bed and breakfasts, or unique boutique accommodations, you'll find plenty of choices throughout the country. Here are some popular accommodation options in the Netherlands:

1. **Hotels:** From internationally renowned hotel chains to charming boutique hotels, the Netherlands has a vast selection of hotels catering to different tastes and budgets. Major cities like Amsterdam, Rotterdam, and The Hague have a wide range of accommodations, including luxury hotels with top-notch amenities and services.
2. **Hostels:** Budget-conscious travelers can opt for hostels, which offer affordable dormitory-style accommodations and often have communal areas where you can meet fellow travelers. Hostels are particularly popular among backpackers and young travelers, and they can be found in major cities as well as smaller towns.
3. **Bed and Breakfasts:** Bed and breakfasts, or B&Bs, provides a cozy and personalized accommodation

experience. They are typically family-run establishments that offer comfortable rooms and a homemade breakfast. B&Bs can be found in various locations across the country, including picturesque countryside settings.
4. **Holiday Rentals:** Vacation rentals, such as apartments, cottages, and villas, are ideal for those seeking a home-away-from-home experience. They offer more space, privacy, and the flexibility to cook your own meals. Many platforms, such as Airbnb, provide a wide range of holiday rental options in different parts of the Netherlands.
5. **Camping:** The Netherlands is known for its well-equipped campsites, making camping a popular accommodation choice for nature lovers. You can find campsites near the coast, in national parks, and in rural areas. Facilities often include showers, toilets, and recreational amenities.

With the diverse range of accommodation options available in the Netherlands, you can find the perfect place to stay that suits your preferences, budget, and desired location. Whether you prefer the comfort of hotels, the social atmosphere of hostels, or the charm of bed and breakfasts, there's something for everyone in the Netherlands.

Local Transportation

The Netherlands offers a well-developed and efficient transportation system that makes it easy to navigate both cities and the countryside. Here are some key aspects of local transportation in the Netherlands:

1. **Public Transportation:** The Netherlands has an extensive network of trains, trams, buses, and metros that connect cities, towns, and rural areas. The national railway company, Nederlandse Spoorwegen (NS), operates frequent train services that are known for their punctuality and reliability. Trams and buses are widely available in major cities, providing convenient transportation within urban areas.
2. **OV-chipkaart:** To use public transportation, it is recommended to have an OV-chipkaart, a contactless smart card that allows you to pay for your journeys. You can top up the card with credit and simply tap it when entering and exiting trains, trams, or buses. The OV-chipkaart can be obtained from ticket machines or service desks at train stations, and it offers discounted fares compared to purchasing individual tickets.

3. **Bicycles:** Cycling is a popular mode of transportation in the Netherlands, and it is a great way to explore cities and towns. Many cities have dedicated cycling lanes and bike rental services available. Bicycles can be rented from various locations, including train stations and dedicated rental shops. It's important to follow traffic rules and be aware of other cyclists and pedestrians while cycling.
4. **Taxis:** Taxis are readily available in cities and can be hailed from designated taxi ranks or booked through taxi apps. It is worth noting that taxis in the Netherlands are metered, and prices can vary, so it's advisable to check the rates before starting your journey.
5. **Driving:** If you plan to rent a car and drive in the Netherlands, it's important to familiarize yourself with local traffic rules and regulations. The road network is well-maintained, and driving allows you to explore more remote areas and smaller towns at your own pace. However, parking can be limited and expensive in city centers, so it's advisable to use park-and-ride facilities or opt for public transportation in urban areas.

Overall, the Netherlands offers a reliable and efficient public transportation system, along with cycling-friendly infrastructure, making it easy to get around and explore the country's vibrant cities and picturesque landscapes.

Communication and Internet Access

Communication and internet access in the Netherlands are highly developed, ensuring that you can stay connected during your visit. Here are some key points to know:

1. **Mobile Networks:** The Netherlands has excellent mobile network coverage, with major providers offering reliable voice and data services. You can choose from prepaid SIM cards or opt for a temporary plan, which allows you to make calls and use data while you're in the country. SIM cards are widely available at airports, electronics stores, and provider outlets.
2. **Internet Access:** Wi-Fi is readily available in hotels, cafes, restaurants, and public spaces throughout the Netherlands. Many accommodations offer free Wi-Fi to guests, and you can also find internet access in public libraries and some train stations. Additionally, there are numerous internet cafes where you can pay for usage by the hour.
3. **International Calls:** If you need to make international calls, it is recommended to check with your mobile service provider for international calling rates or consider using internet-based communication platforms

such as Skype, WhatsApp, or FaceTime, which offer free or low-cost calling and messaging options over Wi-Fi or mobile data.
4. **Language:** Dutch is the official language of the Netherlands. However, English is widely spoken, especially in major cities and tourist areas. You should have no trouble communicating in English with locals, service providers, and in most establishments.

With easy access to mobile networks, widespread Wi-Fi availability, and English proficiency among locals, staying connected and communicating in the Netherlands is convenient and hassle-free. Whether you need to make calls, access the internet, or communicate with locals, you'll have the means to do so during your visit.

Shopping Tips and VAT Refunds

When shopping in the Netherlands, here are some tips to enhance your experience and make the most of your purchases:

1. **Value Added Tax (VAT) Refunds:** Non-EU residents are eligible for a VAT refund on purchases made in the Netherlands. Look for stores displaying a "Tax-Free Shopping" sign and ask for a tax refund form at the time of purchase. At the airport, present the completed form, along with the purchased items, to customs for verification and refund processing.
2. **Opening Hours:** Most shops in the Netherlands are open from Monday to Saturday, with shorter operating hours on Sundays. However, major cities and popular tourist areas often have shops that remain open on Sundays as well. Keep in mind that smaller towns and rural areas may have limited opening hours, especially on weekends.
3. **Popular Shopping Areas:** Amsterdam is renowned for its diverse shopping scene, with popular areas like Kalverstraat, Nine Streets, and the De Bijenkorf department store. Other cities like Rotterdam, The

Updated Netherlands Travel Guide

Hague, and Utrecht also offer a wide range of shopping options, from high-end boutiques to local markets.
4. **Payment Methods:** Credit and debit cards are widely accepted in most shops, restaurants, and hotels in the Netherlands. However, it's always a good idea to carry some cash, especially for smaller establishments and markets that may not accept cards. ATMs are easily accessible throughout the country.
5. **Dutch Specialties:** Don't miss the opportunity to explore Dutch specialties while shopping. From delicious cheeses and stroopwafels (syrup waffles) to Delftware ceramics and local handicrafts, there are unique products that make for great souvenirs or gifts.

By keeping these shopping tips in mind and being aware of VAT refund opportunities, you can make your shopping experience in the Netherlands more enjoyable and rewarding.

Useful Phrases and Translations

While many people in the Netherlands speak English, it's always helpful to learn a few basic Dutch phrases to enhance your travel experience. Here are some useful phrases and translations to assist you:

- Hello - Hallo
- Goodbye - Tot ziens
- Thank you - Dank u (formal) / Dank je (informal)
- Please - Alstublieft (formal) / Alsjeblieft (informal)
- Excuse me - Pardon
- Do you speak English? - Spreekt u Engels? (formal) / Spreek je Engels? (informal)
- I don't understand - Ik begrijp het niet
- Can you help me? - Kunt u mij helpen? (formal) / Kun je me helpen? (informal)
- Where is...? - Waar is...?
- How much does it cost? - Hoeveel kost het?
- I would like... - Ik wil graag...
- Can I have the bill, please? - Mag ik de rekening, alstublieft?
- Cheers! - Proost!

Updated Netherlands Travel Guide

- Excuse me, where is the restroom? - Pardon, waar is het toilet?
- I'm sorry - Het spijt me

These basic phrases will be useful in everyday situations, and locals will appreciate your effort to communicate in their language. Remember, the Dutch are generally friendly and helpful, so don't hesitate to ask for assistance if needed.

INSIDER TIPS AND HIDDEN GEMS

Discovering insider tips and hidden gems can add a touch of magic to your journey through the Netherlands. While the country is known for its iconic attractions, there are lesser-known treasures waiting to be explored. This section provides insights from locals and seasoned travelers, revealing off-the-beaten-path destinations, secret spots, and insider tips to enhance your experience.

Uncover hidden museums, quaint neighborhoods, picturesque canals, and charming cafes that are favored by locals. From hidden gems in Amsterdam to lesser-known towns and natural

Updated Netherlands Travel Guide

wonders, these insider tips will help you go beyond the tourist trail and discover the hidden beauty and unique experiences that the Netherlands has to offer. Get ready to embark on a journey of exploration and uncover the secrets that make the Netherlands truly special.

Off-the-Beaten-Path Destinations

While the Netherlands is famous for its iconic cities and popular attractions, there are numerous off-the-beaten-path destinations that offer a different perspective on the country's beauty and charm. Here are a few worth exploring:

1. **Giethoorn:** Known as the "Venice of the Netherlands," Giethoorn is a picturesque village with no roads. Instead, charming canals and footbridges connect the thatched-roof houses. Rent a boat and navigate the tranquil waterways, or stroll through the village to soak up its idyllic atmosphere.
2. **Kinderdijk:** Located near Rotterdam, Kinderdijk is a UNESCO World Heritage site famous for its iconic windmills. Take a walk or bike ride along the scenic paths that wind through the landscape, and learn about the rich history and engineering behind these impressive structures.
3. **Hoge Veluwe National Park:** Escape to nature at Hoge Veluwe National Park, a vast expanse of heathlands, forests, and sand dunes. Explore the park by bike or on foot, and keep an eye out for wildlife like red deer and wild boar. Don't miss a visit to the Kröller-Müller

Museum, which houses an impressive collection of Van Gogh paintings.
4. **Texel:** As the largest of the Dutch Wadden Islands, Texel offers stunning beaches, charming villages, and unique wildlife. Embark on a bike ride to explore the island's dunes and nature reserves, visit the Ecomare nature center to learn about local marine life and sample fresh seafood at the island's restaurants.
5. **Naarden:** Just a short distance from Amsterdam, Naarden is a well-preserved fortified town with a rich history. Wander through its narrow streets, admire the ancient city walls, and explore the star-shaped fortress. Naarden is also known for its annual classical music festival, attracting musicians and music lovers from around the world.

Venturing off the beaten path in the Netherlands allows you to discover hidden gems, experience the country's natural beauty, and connect with its rich history and culture. These lesser-known destinations offer unique and unforgettable experiences that will leave a lasting impression on your journey.

Unique Experiences in the Netherlands

The Netherlands offers a range of unique experiences that go beyond the typical tourist attractions. Here are a few exceptional experiences to consider during your visit:

1. **Keukenhof Gardens:** Known as the "Garden of Europe," Keukenhof is a vibrant display of tulips and other spring flowers. Explore the meticulously designed gardens, take in the colorful blooms, and witness the beauty of Dutch horticulture. The annual opening of Keukenhof is a highly anticipated event that attracts visitors from around the world.
2. **Windmill Night Photography:** The Netherlands is famous for its windmills, and capturing their beauty at night is a unique experience. Join a guided photography tour to learn the techniques of capturing stunning nighttime shots of windmills against a backdrop of starry skies. It's an opportunity to blend photography skills with the country's iconic symbols.
3. **Dutch Cheese Tasting:** Indulge in a cheese-tasting experience to discover the rich flavors of traditional Dutch cheeses. Visit local cheese farms or specialty shops that offer a wide variety of cheeses, including the

famous Gouda and Edam. Learn about the cheese-making process, sample different types, and pair them with delicious accompaniments like Dutch mustard and stroopwafels.
4. **Canal Cruises in Utrecht:** While Amsterdam is well-known for its canals, Utrecht offers a unique canal experience. Take a leisurely boat cruise through Utrecht's picturesque canals, passing under historic bridges and alongside charming wharf cellars. The peaceful ambiance and beautiful scenery provide a delightful way to explore this enchanting city.
5. **Rotterdam Architecture Tour:** Rotterdam is a modern architectural playground known for its innovative and striking buildings. Embark on an architectural tour to admire the city's skyline, including iconic structures like the Cube Houses, Erasmus Bridge, and the Markthal. Gain insights into Rotterdam's urban development and its transformation into a hub of contemporary architecture.

These unique experiences in the Netherlands allow you to delve deeper into the country's culture, history, and natural beauty. Embrace these opportunities to create lasting memories and a deeper connection with this captivating destination.

CONCLUSION

The Updated Netherlands Travel Guide serves as your comprehensive companion to exploring the diverse and captivating country of the Netherlands. From the iconic canals of Amsterdam to the hidden gems of Rotterdam, The Hague, Utrecht, Maastricht, Groningen, Haarlem, Delft, Leiden, and beyond, this guide is designed to help you make the most of your journey.

Throughout the pages of this guide, you have discovered a wealth of information, ranging from practical tips on planning your trip to in-depth insights into the country's culture, history, and unique offerings. You have learned about the best times to visit, visa requirements, health and safety tips, budgeting and money matters, transportation options, and accommodation choices. You have also delved into the fascinating aspects of Dutch culture, traditions, art, architecture, cuisine, and more.

Updated Netherlands Travel Guide

Whether you seek the vibrant energy of Amsterdam's nightlife, the tranquility of Dutch parks and outdoor activities, the immersion into the country's rich history through museums and landmarks, or the exploration of lesser-known towns and off-the-beaten-path destinations, the Netherlands has something for every traveler.

By embracing the local customs and etiquette, engaging with the friendly locals, and trying traditional delicacies, you can create a more meaningful and authentic experience. From cycling through picturesque landscapes to indulging in canal cruises and savoring Dutch cheeses, the Netherlands offers a plethora of unique adventures and memories waiting to be made.

This travel guide aims to provide you with accurate and up-to-date information, allowing you to navigate the country with confidence and discover the true essence of the Netherlands. Whether you are a first-time visitor or a seasoned traveler, this guide will assist you in planning a remarkable and unforgettable trip.

As you embark on your journey through the Netherlands, remember to embrace the spirit of adventure, curiosity, and appreciation for the country's rich heritage. Immerse yourself in the vibrant cities, explore the enchanting countryside, and allow yourself to be captivated by the warmth and charm of the Dutch people.

The Updated Netherlands Travel Guide hopes to serve as a valuable resource, igniting your passion for travel and inspiring you to embark on an extraordinary exploration of this remarkable country. May your time in the Netherlands be filled with unforgettable experiences, lifelong memories, and a deep appreciation for the beauty and diversity that awaits you.

Enjoy your travels through the Netherlands, and may this guide be your trusted companion every step of the way!

Updated Netherlands Travel Guide

Can You Do Me A Favor?

Are you one of the thousands of people who have read my book in the Updated Netherlands Travel Guide? If so, I'd love to hear your thoughts! Please take a few moments to drop a review on Amazon and let me know what you think. Your opinion matters, and I'm sure your review will help others decide if this book is right for them. Thank you so much for being a part of this journey.

With sincere gratitude,

Lucas Everhart.

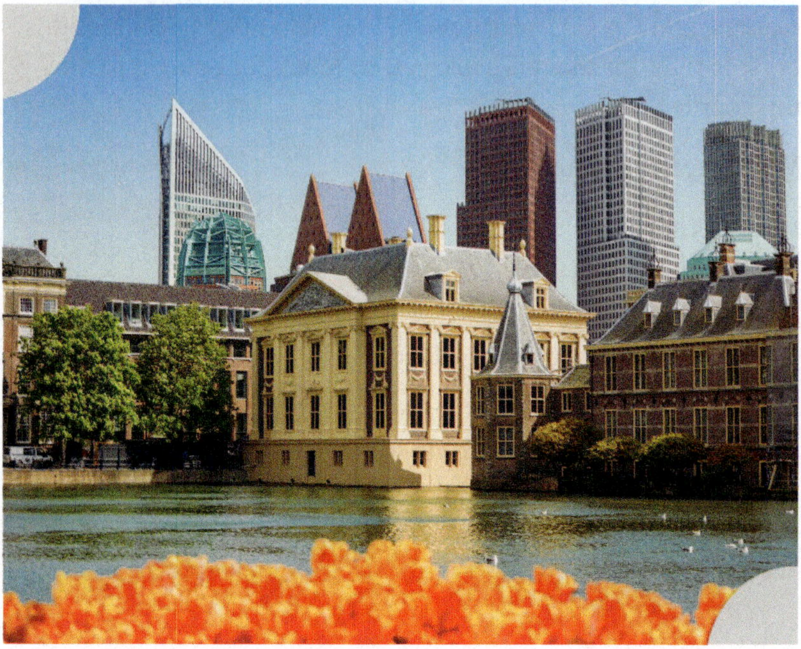

Printed in Great Britain
by Amazon

40713026R00066